T0207572

SIMPLE SIGNS OF GOD'S LOVE

JUDYANN KRELL MORSE

WESTBOW
PRESS®
A DIVISION OF THOMAS NELSON
& ZONDERVAN

WestBow Press books may be ordered through booksellers or by contacting:

WestBow Press
A Division of Thomas Nelson & Zondervan
1663 Liberty Drive
Bloomington, IN 47403
www.westbowpress.com
844-714-3454

Because of the dynamic nature of the Internet, any web addresses or links contained in this book may have changed since publication and may no longer be valid. The views expressed in this work are solely those of the author and do not necessarily reflect the views of the publisher, and the publisher hereby disclaims any responsibility for them.

Any people depicted in stock imagery provided by Getty Images are models, and such images are being used for illustrative purposes only. Certain stock imagery © Getty Images.

Scripture quotations marked (KJV) are take nfrom the King James Version of the Bible.

Scripture quotations marked (NIV) are taken from the Holy Bible, New International Version®. NIV®. Copyright © 1973, 1978, 1984, 2011 by Biblica, Inc.® Used by permission of Zondervan All rights reserved worldwide. www.zondervan.com The "NIV" and "New International Version" are trademarks registered in the United States Patent and Trademark Office by Biblica, Inc.®

Scripture marked (NKJV) taken from the New King James Version®. Copyright © 1982 by Thomas Nelson. Used by permission. All rights reserved.

Scripture quotations marked (NLT) are taken from the Holy Bible, New Living Translation, copyright ©1996, 2004, 2015 by Tyndale House Foundation. Used by permission of Tyndale House Publishers, a Division of Tyndale House Ministries, Carol Stream, Illinois 60188. All rights reserved.

Scripture quotations marked (TLB) are taken from The Living Bible copyright © 1971. Used by permission of Tyndale House Publishers, a Division of Tyndale House Ministries, Carol Stream, Illinois 60188. All rights reserved.

ISBN: 978-1-6642-1037-0 (sc)
ISBN: 978-1-6642-1038-7 (hc)
ISBN: 978-1-6642-1036-3 (e)

Library of Congress Control Number: 2020921112

Print information available on the last page.

WestBow Press rev. date: 11/06/2020

To my Dad,

The Rev. Richard A. Krell,

a man who lived a life of faith every day.

INTRODUCTION

How do I tell you about the book you are holding? First, it wasn't written in a just a week, a month, or even a year. Rather, it was written over five decades in moments between sending my older sons off to elementary school and giving my newborn son a bath, moments when a simple sign of God's love would filter into my consciousness.

Grabbing a pen and scrap of paper, I would scribble down a few words, fully intending to return and "flesh them out" into a devotional, which didn't happen. Instead, those scribbled thoughts joined others in folders and notebooks that were filed away to be worked on at a later time.

Finally, fifty years later, that time has arrived; the scribbled thoughts have been pulled from the folders and notebooks and compiled into the book in your hand

This is not a book that must be read from front to back; it can be started from any page. And as you do so, it is my hope that the stories found in these pages will remind you that God is always present in both the dramatic and the mundane events of life. Wherever you start reading, I hope you will accept this book for what it is meant to be: a prompt to recognize the simple signs of God's love in your life.

JudyAnn Krell Morse

MY SINCERE THANKS TO:

Rev. Richard A. Krell: Dad, you were more than a parent; you were my role model, counselor, adviser, and friend.

Greg Loose: You were the first to read my scribbled thoughts and pronounce them worth publishing.

Carol Kimball: As my trusted friend for over fifty years, you have guided me through days of sheer happiness and deep sadness.

Marilyn Simmons: Dear friend, you put music, joy, and laughter into all the days of my life, even as you continually lift me up in prayer.

Jo Ann Wiele: Gone but not forgotten. Your gifts of wisdom and counsel helped me become a stronger person of faith and a better pastor.

Marilyn Krell: Beloved sister-in-law, your demonstration of faith in tough times continues to inspire me.

To the First UCC Congregation: Together we worked hard and prayed harder in serving the Lord.

To the special women in my life (you know who you are!), who take my phone calls and give of yourself whenever I need help: I thank you!

To my firstborn son, Alan Berg: Thank you for calling to say you love me so often and reassuring me that I was, and still am, a good mother!

To my son and daughter-in-law, Richard and Penny Berg: Thanks for your love and faith in me, and helping turn my dream of becoming a published author into a reality.

And to my husband of thirty years, Delbert Morse: Thank you, dear husband, for picking me up, dusting me off, and making life turn out right.

I am blessed!

TIME TO ADJUST
THE ATTITUDE

I press toward the mark.
—Philippians 3:14 (KJV)

With my fiftieth birthday just a few days away, I fired up my Yamaha 650 motorcycle to ride from Burlington, Iowa, to my parents' home in Oshkosh, Wisconsin, to celebrate. It was a perfect September day to ride, with sunshine and brilliant fall colors filling the Iowa landscape. But as I crossed the Mississippi River at Dubuque into Wisconsin for the last leg of the 350-mile ride, the sun began to set, and temperatures began to fall. I stopped several times to pull on a turtleneck, heavier jacket, and gloves. And I began to groan and moan about how cold it was getting.

Fifty miles later, I was downright hostile! "What radar conditions prompted that weatherman to predict warm temperatures until midnight?" I grumbled. "If these are warm temperatures, I certainly would hate to experience cold ones!"

And that's when I saw the huge black-and-white sign in the middle of the corn field: "Attitude Adjustment Hour 4–5 p.m." That's all it said.

"Yeah, that's just what I need right now!" I laughed. "An attitude adjustment hour. I need to clean up my act and be thankful for an uneventful ride instead of complain about how cold it is! For hasn't my cycle purred along smoothly for over two hundred miles? Hasn't the road been free of obstacles and construction? Did I *really* think it was going to stay warm until midnight? Seriously?"

I often whine about situations in my spiritual life as well. Life hands me challenges, and I moan and groan about them instead of taking them to God in prayer and asking for His guidance. I need to take to heart the words that the apostle Paul wrote in verses 13 and 14 of Philippians: "But one thing I do. Forgetting what lies behind … I press on toward the goal for the prize of the upward call of God in Christ Jesus" (Philippians 3:13–14 ESV).

Starting today, I will make it a point to whine less and pray more.

Do you also need to see a sign announcing an attitude adjustment to quiet your grumbling and remind you of God's love and protection in your life?

Prayer

Thank You, Father, for reminders of Your love in the most unlikely places. May we recognize them and allow them to draw us closer to You. Amen.

COMFORT FOODS

Cheerfully share your home.

—1 Peter 4:9 (NLT)

It had been a difficult week with two funerals, troublesome sermon preparation, challenging Bible-study research, and being just plain tired. So when a friend called to invite me to her home for lunch the next day, I accepted, even though I doubted that I would be good company.

The following day she welcomed me into her home and led me into the warm and cozy kitchen. Assuring me that she hadn't gone to any trouble to make the meal, she brought out homemade macaroni and cheese, crispy chicken strips from the oven, and a bowl of her very own applesauce from the fridge. Unbeknown to her, she had just set three of my all-time favorite comfort foods on the table and had done so with cheerfulness and joy.

As we ate the delicious food and shared news of our family and friends, the tension that I had experienced earlier in the day faded away, and it was replaced with a sense of peace.

As I opened my Bible the following morning to begin my devotions, my eyes filled with tears as I read the verse of the day from 1 Peter 4, that appears at the beginning of this chapter. I closed my eyes and thanked God that He had once again shown me, through the actions of a special friend, how important it is to "cheerfully share your home." As a result of her hospitality, my soul was soothed, and my attitude was improved.

> I'm ready to invite others into our home
> joyfully. Would you like to come visit?

Prayer

> Dear Father, thank You for friends who accept us as we are and who make our lives better through their kindness and compassion. Help me learn from their actions that I, too, may be a gracious hostess to those in need. These things I pray in Jesus' Name. Amen.

GETTING INTO
THE SPIRIT

For it's not where we worship that counts, but how
we worship—is our worship spiritual and real? Do
we have the Holy Spirit's help? For God is Spirit, and
we must have His help to worship as we should.
—John 4:23, 24 (TLB, emphasis added)

Have you ever had one of those Sundays when you just couldn't
get into the spirit of worship? I have! The sermon seemed boring,
the service was endless, and I couldn't find a comfortable way to sit
still. And why was that? Perhaps I had spent too many extra hours
working earlier in the week or stayed up too late on Saturday
night. Maybe I was feeling the pressure of being unprepared for
a project due in the coming week. Any or all of these things may
have factored into my restlessness. But the biggest difficulty was
that I had not mentally or spiritually prepared myself to worship.

During the organ prelude, had I ceased talking and instead
bowed my head to ask the Holy Spirit to guide me through the
worship service? Isn't that one of the purposes of the prelude—to
direct my thoughts away from myself and toward God whom I
have come to worship? Isn't it true that we *must* have His (God's)
help to worship as we should? Yes, it is true. Doing so will make
our time in worship more fulfilling.

In future worship services, I'm ready to include a word of prayer during the prelude as my preparation for worship.

Will you join me?

Prayer

Dear Father, I'm sorry for all the times I have been unprepared to worship and praise You. Nudge me to include You in my time of preparation for worship. In Your Name I pray.

MOUTH SHUT AND LIPS SEALED

Help me, Lord, to keep my mouth shut and my lips sealed.

—Psalm 141:3 (TLB)

In the past I have been totally uncomfortable with discussions at several committee meetings. I had opinions on the topic of discussion but knew that what I had to say was better left unsaid. Feelings would be hurt, and perhaps dissention would rear its ugly head. At those times, I silently asked God to put His hand over my mouth to keep me silent when I was prone to speak.

Imagine my great joy during a recent morning devotional to find that the writer of the Psalm 141 must have shared my challenge. "Help me, Lord," he wrote, "to keep my mouth shut and my lips sealed."

Seeing this prayer written out by someone far wiser than me has helped me to know that I am not alone in speaking when I should be silent. Finding it written in Psalms has reassured me that this is a centuries-old challenge that has plagued many individuals before me.

But being aware of this will not stop the challenge from repeating itself in the future. There will still be times when I will want to say things that are better left unsaid. At those moments, I will remember the prayer written by the psalmist and rest assured that God will hear and answer my prayer when, and if, I pray it.

I'm ready to ask for God's help in this area. Is this an area where you need help too?

Prayer

Dear Father, help me to remember that once words are spoken they can never be retrieved. Be with me and keep me silent when the words are best left unsaid. This I pray in Jesus' Name. Amen.

DOWN MEMORY LANE

Call to remembrance the former days.

—Hebrews 10:32 (KJV)

In recent days I have been sorting through boxes and boxes of photographs from earlier years of my life. Doing so has taken me down memory lanes to the years when my three grown sons were boys still living at home. I came across a picture of my oldest son, Alan, playing with our dog, Benny. Another showed my middle son, Ken, wearing his Boy Scout uniform and carrying the flag in the Labor Day parade. And there was my youngest son, Rich, riding a merry-go-round. Other pictures showed all three boys perched at the top of a slide in the park or leaning against the station wagon during one of our day trips. Gathered together, these pictures reminded me of the long-ago days when my sons were young schoolboys, learning to swim, riding bicycles, and going to their first dances.

I could lose myself for hours going back through these pictures and reliving those memories. For the days when our family took long walks in the pines and huddled around the living room fireplace roasting marshmallows were good days that are forever indelibly etched in the fiber of my being.

Today when I look at my sons, I see boys who have grown into strong men. I see men who have set goals and achieved them, who work hard to earn an honest day's pay, and who show respect for their family and friends. And it is then that I not only thank God for the gift of memory—the ability to "call to remembrance the former days"—but also for the gift of time during which I have watched my sons grow into the fine men they are.

> I dust off the cobwebs of yesteryear and
> smile at the remembrances.
> And I invite you to do the same.

Prayer

> Thank You, Father, for precious years with my sons and for the ability to remember them. May I always give thanks for my sons and the important roles they have played in my life. I pray this in the Name of Jesus. Amen.

ONLY TWELVE

Thus sayeth the Lord unto you, be not afraid
nor dismayed by reason of the great multitude;
for the battle is not yours, but God's.

—2 Chronicles 20:15 (KJV)

Only twelve people sat in the pews on that Sunday morning several years ago. Twelve people who had watched friends and extended family members leave this congregation to worship elsewhere because of difficulties with former pastors and other church members.

And as I stood before them to preach, I was fearful of those who had left for they were the ones who were telling the twelve that this congregation could not survive. Those who had left were predicting failure for those who had stayed behind to carry on the traditions and the mission of the church.

And in all honesty, neither the remaining twelve nor I were certain that the church *would* survive. But then I read the verse from 2 Chronicles, shown above:" Do not fear … for the battle is not yours but God's". There was no doubt in my mind that we had a battle on our hands, which would involve developing a spirit of forgiveness and a positive attitude. Many people had suffered spiritual and emotional wounds that would not be easily healed. But believing that all things are possible when we put our trust in God, we resolved to look to God for strength and courage, and then look forward to healing wounds and growing a church.

Today, forty to fifty people gather to worship. Sadly, the majority of those first twelve have gone to be with the Lord; new individuals have taken their places. As we remember those twelve "pioneers" who worked hard and prayed harder, we thank God for leading us forward to victory in Him.

> Don't let a small number discourage you;
> remember, Jesus started with twelve disciples.

Prayer

> Thank You, God, for timeless words from Your Holy Word, which give us courage to face the challenges of life and move forward without fear. Amen.

A VALENTINE FOR GOD?

For God so loved the world that He
gave His Only Begotten Son.

—John 3:16 (KJV)

This morning I left home with a list in my hand of valentines I needed to purchase. Standing in front of the rack, I panicked for a moment; there were so many choices to look through to find just the right ones. I needed an extra-special one for my husband, three for my sons, one for granddaughter Kaili, one for Uncle Fred, and … Well, my list had several more names on it. With Valentine's Day just a week away, I was congratulating myself on the prospect of mailing my cards on time this year. But as I paid for my purchases, I got to wondering what a valentine to God might look like. Since we send valentines to those we love and admire, shouldn't God be on this list too?

Where did that thought come from? I wondered as I started the drive back home. "Send a valentine to God? Impossible! Can't be done!"

Or can it? Loving others as He has loved me would be one way I could turn my life into a valentine for God. And forgiving others as He has forgiven me is another way of showing my love for Him. Doing these things won't always be easy, I know. However, God has loved me many times when I was not very lovable and has forgiven me more times than I could ever count. So it's worth a try, isn't it?

So you see, it *is* possible to give God a valentine by putting His love into action and making it real.

If we all turned our lives into valentines to
God, the world would be a better place.

Prayer

Father, fill me with Your love and forgiveness that
I may share it with others. Amen.

DID I CATCH ANY FISH?

For the water turns to ice as hard as rock,
and the surface of the water freezes.

—Job 38:30 (NLT)

Shortly after we started dating, the man who is now my husband called and invited me to go ice fishing. Considering that my idea of winter entertainment was reading a good book while sipping hot chocolate, I was very tempted to say no. But since making a good impression on him overrode my laziness, the next Saturday found me dressed in many layers of socks and heavy clothing, waddling toward a frozen farm pond with a Styrofoam box of wax worms in my pocket and a fishing pole in my hand. I am so glad that I went on that first ice-fishing date with him! Standing there on that frozen pond in the absolute hush of God's creation, I could be still and know that God was there. Gone was the frenzy of office life; gone were the extra tensions of multitasking while finishing complicated projects; gone was the compulsion to live up to the expectations of others while ignoring my own hopes and goals. All of that faded from my thoughts as I became totally enveloped by the nearness of the God of creation. My mind stilled, and my soul rested. Did I catch any fish? I don't remember! What I do remember is that while standing in the frigid temperatures on the frozen farm pond, I communed with God in a new way that day and on countless other days of ice fishing since then. And each time I stood on the ice, I truly felt that "Surely the Lord is in this place; and I knew it not" (Genesis 28:16 NIV).

I found God in a most unlikely and unexpected place. And I am a better person for it.

Have you found God in any new places in life lately?

Prayer

> Thank You, God, for meeting us in unexpected situations and places. Amen.

I CONFESS ...

And why beholdest thou the mote that is in thy brother's eye, but perceivest not the beam that is in thine own eye?

—Luke 6:41 (KJV)

The damage had been done. One of my young sons had gotten hold of their father's paintbrush and did some unauthorized painting in the living room. And now it was my responsibility to find out which child had done so.

Calling both boys, then ages three and four, into their bedroom, I calmly told them that I was very disappointed that one of them had disobeyed his father by painting on the wall. Because this was very serious, the guilty one would have to sit on a chair for an hour while I fixed supper. Then I asked the guilty one to confess. What *was* I thinking?

The boys stood silently in front of me. And I waited, determined to sit there as long as it took to get a confession from the guilty party. Soon the wait got long for my sons, and they began to wiggle and move from side to side. And still I waited.

Once again, I asked the guilty child to confess; once again silence reigned supreme. Wanting to add a bit more pressure, I said, "Well since neither of you are going to own up to this wrongdoing, I guess both of you will have to take the punishment. Instead of sitting on the chair for an hour, both of you will need to come in and put your pajamas on right after supper and go to bed. Neither of you will be allowed to go out and play on the swings before bedtime."

Again they stood silent—until four-year-old Alan quietly spoke up: "Okay, Mom, I confess. [Long silent pause] Kenneth did it!"

Like my son, I am often more willing to "confess" for others instead of owning up to my own shortcomings.

> Courage to confess our own shortcomings,
> rather than those of others,
> will bring us closer to God.

Prayer

> Thank You, God, for children who, in their innocence, put laughter in our lives. Amen.

FIRST THING IN
THE MORNING

He wakeneth morning by morning; He
wakeneth mine ear to hear.

—Isaiah 50:4 (KJV)

Why is it that some of my most productive ideas come in the first
few minutes after I wake up? Solutions to challenges I have been
struggling with for ages seem to just pop into my head. Names of
friends come to mind whom I need to send notes off to or return
a call made to me at an earlier time. I almost look forward to
waking up to discover what marvelous thoughts are waiting for
me. Why, I have even gotten some devotional ideas in those first
waking moments. Why do you think this is?

Do you suppose that this is the only time that God has my
full attention and is able to communicate with me? I often preach
about communing with God in prayer. Doesn't it make sense
that God also likes to commune with me when He answers my
prayers?

Thinking more about this, I began to understand that God
does have a difficult time getting my attention. With all the noise
around me, the hectic schedule, the time spent shopping, and
sharing lunch with friends, all those telephone calls and letters and
cards I love to write, where do I leave time for listening to God?

This is a totally new concept that I want to explore more fully in hopes of realizing its full potential. Come to think about it, Jesus often got up early in the morning and went away from His disciples to pray and commune with God. This time spent in prayer opened up the lines of communication between God and His Son. I believe I will do the same. From now on, I am going to listen first to any messages God may be sending me and then give thanks in prayer.

Have you tried praying first thing in the morning?
It will make the day go better.

Prayer

Thank You, Father, for opening my mind to new lessons You are teaching me. Nudge me to put them into practice so that I may draw closer to You. This I ask in Jesus' Name. Amen.

WRITE IT BY HAND

Each of you should use whatever gift you have received to serve others, as faithful stewards of God's grace in its various forms.

—1 Peter 4:10–11 (NIV)

In this age of e-mail and electronic messaging, I have to admit that I miss the good old days when my mailbox held handwritten letters and cards from family and friends. I miss handwritten Christmas cards that share news about new babies and vacation trips.

Oh, yes, sending e-mails and messaging is quicker and more efficient than snail mail and handwritten notes. But greetings sent through the mail are tangible; I can tuck them away to be read again and again, which is why I miss receiving them so much.

That's why I am so grateful for the ministry of a good friend in our church who regularly—weekly—sends out cards to those who are ill, have lost a loved one, or facing one of life's challenges. Because of the time she spends selecting just the right card, and then writing a friendly note on it before mailing it out, many people have been encouraged and reminded that they are not alone. They have a friend who took the time to send a card.

I am going to try harder to follow the example of this lady who ministers to others with greeting cards. She is touching the lives of others through her greeting card ministry.

Are we, in like manner, using the gifts God has given us to share His love with others?

Prayer

Dear Father, we often overlook the everyday gifts and talents You have given us when we reach out to others. Show us today how to serve You better. In Jesus' Name, Amen.

TOO TIRED TO PRAY

O Lord, my God, I cried to Thee for
help, and Thou hast healed me.

—Psalm 30:2 (KJV)

I had no idea an earache could hurt so much. But the one that hit me on Saturday and carried over into Sunday was almost more pain than I could bear.

An incorrect diagnosis at a local clinic on Monday resulted in being treated for five days for a nonexistent ear infection. During this time, the left side of my face "fell," leaving me with the appearance of a stroke victim. Finally, on Friday at my insistence, I was examined by another physician who correctly diagnosed Bell's Palsy. I cried all the way home.

"Oh, God, looking like this, I will never be able to clown again. I worked so hard to perfect the personality of Sonshine the Clown to share the love of Jesus with children and their families. And now, my eight years as Sonshine are ending. And how will I ever preach again? I can't stand up in front of people looking like this!"

I took to my bed in the darkened bedroom, crying out my pain and frustration to God. And then I slept. For days on end I sobbed, I slept, and I cried out to God. I couldn't see light at the end of this tunnel. My spiritual journey had taken a definite left turn and was taking me into new and uncharted waters.

And when I was too tired and spent to pray any longer, my family and friends lifted me up to God in prayer. Individuals in at least five states were praying daily for my return to good health and further service in the pulpit. Their prayers, and mine, were answered. Over the next five months, slowly but surely, the muscles in my face were strengthened. My smile is not the same, and I have some difficulty with my eye. But all in all, my health and my face were restored. And although I no longer serve as Sonshine the Clown, God has blessed me with the privilege of serving a church as its pastor.

I know from experience that God answers prayers. Have you experienced this too?

Prayer

> Thank You, Father, for hearing and answering all prayers that are sincerely prayed. Help us to know that even our faintest cries are heard by You. In Jesus' Name we pray. Amen.

CAN YOU SEE ME?

Thou, O God, didst send a plentiful rain.

—Psalm 68:9 (KJV)

While riding my motorcycle south from Bayfield to Sparta in Wisconsin, it started to rain. So I pulled off to seek shelter under an overpass and to put on my rain gear. Back on the road a few minutes later, what had been a light shower became a drenching downpour with decreased visibility, creating a serious challenge for me. Since I could barely see the taillights of the car ahead, I was concerned that perhaps I had become almost invisible to the driver of the vehicle behind me. Which raised the question, should I pull over and wait out the downpour, thus becoming a sitting target for a passing motorist? Or continue moving with the traffic and hope that my taillights announced my presence to anyone getting too close?

I elected to continue riding in the hard rain, talking out loud to God a lot during those long miles. Over an hour later, I rode safely into Sparta as the sun began to peek out through the clouds.

As I thought about this experience later, I realized that I have experienced storms in my spiritual life as well. Difficult chapters of my life have brought storms that often obscured the path of my spiritual journey. And when I have lost my way or became unsure of what God's plan was for me, I have talked to Him about it, just as I did during the rainstorm on my motorcycle. And I can honestly say that even though life's storms have rained down upon me many times, God has always been there to protect me and lead me forward to brighter days.

Has this been your experience as well?

Prayer

God, it is so easy to get lost on our spiritual journey during the storms of life. Give us faith to trust You for guidance as we journey on life's roads. In Jesus' Name we pray. Amen.

WHY SAVE THEM?

A time to keep, and a time to cast away.

—Ecclesiastes 3:6 (KJV)

I've seen it far too many times, and I've done it myself ... saving the "good" china and silverware for company and holidays. But why do we do this? Oh, yes, the china is more fragile than our everyday tableware, and we certainly don't want to lose a piece of the good silver. But when it comes right down to the bottom line, what *are* we saving it for?

Some would suggest that well, that's what Grandma and Mom did, so we are just following a tradition. And I know this is true because that was the tradition in our family too. But when one's life is over, and the china and silverware are pulled out of their safe and secure storage spots, will they mean as much and be as highly treasured by our next of kin as they were to us? Will they appreciate the time and effort we spent choosing just the right patterns to complement our table settings? Shouldn't we be using them now, when *we* can enjoy them?

Which brings me to another treasure in our lives that is often kept in a safe spot in our homes: God's Holy Word, the Bible. Many times it, too, is pulled out and used only in a special situation, like when we're ill, experiencing one of life's big challenges, or trying to find some peace after losing a loved one or dear friend. This Book was meant to offer us direction, guidance, and comfort each and every day of our lives. Sadly, we do not use it this way; instead, we often ignore it until life has challenged us. But this habit can be changed, starting today. We can open the Bible anytime, day or night, and gain new insight for our spiritual lives.

God *is* still speaking through His Holy
Word. If you believe this,
start reading your Bible daily, and hear
what God has to say to you.

Prayer

Dear Father, today my ears are open to hear Your voice through the words of scripture. Speak, Lord, for I am listening. Amen.

SERVE YOU
WHERE, LORD?

And who knoweth whether thou art come to
the kingdom for such a time as this?
—Esther 4:14 (KJV)

I have always known that I wanted to serve the Lord in some capacity. I have tried to walk through any door of service He opened for me; a Sunday school class needed a teacher; the youth director needed a chaperone for the skating party; the pastor asked for a volunteer to serve as his worship assistant. Many times the call to serve was easy to identify. Other times, the path was more difficult to discern.

One of those times came soon after I turned fifty. I grew restless and began to question my work in the Lord's kingdom. "Is this it, Lord? Is this all that You have for me to do? An occasional Sunday morning message here? A woman's retreat meditation there? Lord, I had so hoped to have more opportunities to speak for You and share Your love with others."

God heard my continual prayers in this matter, and doors of opportunity began to open. Two churches who shared one pastor called to invite me to preach each Sunday for six months while they finalized the calling of a new pastor. Two weeks before that six-month period was up, a congregation in a neighboring town called and extended a similar invitation as they, too, were finalizing the calling of a new pastor to their pulpit.

And then, two weeks before that period of service ended, an opportunity to enroll in a three-year-course of study arose that would enable me to become a licensed pastor with full rights to baptize, officiate at weddings, and serve the sacrament of Holy Communion.

I completed that course of study and was called to be the pastor of a small but growing congregation. And as I sit in the quiet sanctuary in the early morning hours to pray for guidance, I feel truly blest as I offer words of deep gratitude for the opportunity to serve the Lord in this place and in this way. For like Esther in the verse quoted above, I truly feel that "I was created for such a time as this."

Have you sought God's guidance as you, too, seek to discern His will for your life?

Prayer

> Thank You, Father, for this awesome opportunity
> to labor for You in this place. Amen.

SHE MADE US FEEL SPECIAL

Dorcas … who was always doing good and
helping the poor … became sick and died.

—Acts 9:36 (NIV)

Her parents ran the restaurant at the local truck stop, which is where she learned to cook as a teenager. Many were the burgers she fried up and the roast beef and mashed potato platters she served. Slowly but surely she grew to know without looking at a recipe just how many burgers could be made out of a pound of ground beef and how many servings of mashed potatoes would be needed for fifty platters the following day.

Her experience in the truck stop kitchen proved invaluable when she became the chairperson of the church Kitchen Ministry Committee. If a fellowship meal was to be served to eighty people, she knew how many pounds of roast beef should be ordered. If hot chicken casserole was on the menu for a family meal following a memorial service, she could go to the store and buy just the right amount of chicken. She had a wealth of information tucked away in her mind that she freely shared to make every church meal a success.

But this isn't what made her so special. This isn't what brought over three hundred people to the church for the memorial service following her death from cancer before she was sixty.

It was the way she made each of us feel special, the way she looked out for us when life had mowed us down. It was her kind and gentle way of giving of herself and her limited financial resources to remind us that we always had a friend we could count on in both good and difficult times.

Like Dorcas in the Bible verse quoted above, she was always doing good, helping not only the poor of the world but those of us who were often poor in spirit as well. In her short life, she taught the rest of us that lives *can* be changed through the deeds of one person. She lived her faith and changed the world.

Can the same be said about our lives?

Prayer

> Dear Father, You have called each one of us to share Your love with others. Now give us courage to go forth and live our faith. In Jesus' Name we pray. Amen.

ME, INSPIRED?

All Scripture is given by inspiration by God.

—2 Timothy 3:16 (KJV)

During my course of study to become a licensed pastor, I encountered a professor whom I will call Betty (not her real name). In her first lecture, Betty questioned the accuracy and authenticity of the Bible, wondering aloud if there were, in fact, myths, fables, and less-than-accurate accounts of events detailed in the Bible. As I listened, I became highly agitated. After ten minutes, I could sit still no longer. I raised my hand to speak, and when she acknowledged me, I began, "I believe that the Bible is the inspired Word of God and—"

Betty promptly interrupted me. "What *exactly* does that mean?

"I believe it means that God put His thoughts into the minds of humans who then recorded those thoughts."

"You're a pastor, right?" she fired back. "When you write a sermon, are you inspired by God?"

I hesitated. "Well I certainly don't put myself in the same class as Isaiah, Moses, or Paul."

"So you're *not* inspired by God when you write a sermon?"

Wishing I hadn't started this discussion, I stammered on. "I pray a lot while I'm writing a sermon. And I can tell by the way the sermon evolves whether I am on the right track. If I get in the middle, and the sermon just won't go any further, then I figure I am not delivering the right message, so I back up and try again."

"So," Betty said with a big smile, "are you saying that you *are* inspired by God?"

Fortunately, one of my seventeen classmates raised a question and took the heat off me. But for weeks, perhaps months, Betty's question lurked in my mind, raising its ugly head every time I stepped into the pulpit. Was I inspired?

Later, after seeking advice from a more experienced pastor, I was reminded that since God has led me to the pulpit to serve Him, I had best put Betty's words out of my mind and focus on God and the message He had given me to share.

And the lesson I learned from this?

> I must do the work set before me with
> the God-given talents I possess,
> and do it for the glory of God.

Prayer

> Dear Father, when doing Your work, we often get sidetracked by the opinions of others. Remind us that it is Your opinion that matters the most. Inspire us, Lord, so that we make a difference. Amen.

SIMPLE, YET PROFOUND

If any of you lack wisdom, let him ask of God.

—James 1:5 (KJV)

His name was Ashley. He was an unmarried man who cared for his aged mother while farming the Iowa land that had been in his family for generations. On this night, more than fifty years ago, the weekly Thursday night Bible study had concluded, and it was time for prayer. Ashley, along with other members of the Mineral Ridge Baptist Church, was down on his knees and leaning on a pew. Most of those who usually prayed out loud had done so, and the room was quiet. The time had come for the pastor to end the evening with his prayer. But for some reason, he hesitated.

And that's when Ashley, who had never before prayed aloud in the Bible study he had attended for decades, quietly shared what sounded like an urgent prayer request: "Dear Lord … make me wise … but keep me humble. Amen."

One could almost hear the gasps of astonishment because Ashley had prayed aloud. The pastor even sounded a bit surprised as he concluded the evening with prayer before everyone stood and departed.

I have never forgotten that ten-word prayer that was uttered that night. In fact, I have repeated those ten words often in my own prayer life. For even though Ashley's prayer on that long-ago night was simple and brief, its content was powerful, meaningful, and unforgettable. And thus, Ashley's simple prayer taught me an important lesson:

It isn't the length of the prayer that matters, it is the sincerity.

Prayer

God, I too pray this day that You will make me wise but keep me humble. Amen.

SMOKY MOUNTAIN
MORNING

And seeing the multitudes, He went up into a mountain.

—Matthew 5:1 (KJV)

There is a very special place in my heart for the Smoky Mountains of Tennessee. Perhaps these feeling stems from the memory of a September morning on Hummingbird Hill outside of Gatlinburg.

It hadn't been my plan at bedtime to be up at such an early hour; in fact, I had hoped to sleep in until at least 9:00. But sleep had eluded me; I had tossed and turned while wrestling with feelings of anxiety and frustration. My life was all mixed up: A colleague had not lived up to my expectations, my job was eating me alive, and frustration from a serious delay in our travel plans the previous day gnawed at the edges of my soul. Unwilling to toss and turn any longer, I silently threw on jeans, a sweatshirt, and shoes and crept silently from the cabin, leaving my husband sleeping peacefully in the warm cabin.

Outside, as the predawn chill surrounded me, I became aware of the total silence around me. I felt as if I was the only creature alive as not even a bird was chirping to greet the dawn. And it was then, as I sat physically shivering on a cold metal lawn chair, that the presence of God began to warm my heart. For in the total stillness of that Smoky Mountain morning, I knew beyond all doubt that God was there with me, erasing the hurt, anger, and disappointments and replacing them with the peace that only He can give.

Jesus Himself often went to a mountaintop to feel closer to God as He prayed and meditated. And now I know why! The nearness of God on a mountaintop frees the mind and spirit to commune with Him more easily, and ponder and plan the day about to begin.

Have you ventured outside to commune with God in the early morning stillness?

Prayer

> Thank You, God, for being with me that morning
> and every morning of my life! Amen.

LOOKING BEYOND
THE FLAWS

Create in me a clean heart, O God, and
renew a right spirit within me.

—Psalm 51:10 (KJV)

Stacked up in a corner of the basement, those rough boards just looked like a pile of lumber to me. Looking at rough corners, splintery edges, and surface imperfections, I could see no beauty in it whatsoever. But my husband looked beyond the roughness and envisioned the bigger picture of a piece of furniture for our home.

Hour by hour and evening by evening he sawed, planed, and sanded. And slowly his vision evolved into reality. Many months later, using his patience, skill, and vision, he created and then carried a one-of-a-kind curio cabinet from his basement woodshop up to the living room, a curio cabinet in which I proudly display my collectible treasures. A year or two later, an entertainment center he designed was brought into the living room to hold the television and stereo. And two years later, a slant-front desk complete with inside drawers and a secret compartment was moved into the dining room. Each of these pieces, plus several more, has been expertly crafted from rough lumber by my husband's skilled hands.

In like manner, my life has many imperfections and flaws that are easily seen by others. I'm hesitant to give in when I think I'm right. I expect others to live up to my expectations, which isn't fair to them. And I have a temper that often gets me into trouble.

Thankfully, God envisions the bigger picture of my life. Daily—hourly—He sands and smoothes my imperfections with His love and forgiveness, giving me the opportunity to move forward with the new look of a forgiven child of God. And while I will never achieve perfection in this life, I am still being molded by the skilled hands of my heavenly Father, whose only Son grew up in a carpenter's shop during His time here on earth.

In God's eyes, I am a work in progress.
And the same can be said of each of His children.

Prayer

Dear Father, You know how slow I am to admit that I have failed or fallen short of Your expectations. Thank You for continuing to work with me, allowing me to grow in my faith. Amen.

A WARM WELCOME

You make known to me the path of life.

—Psalm 16:11 (NIV)

This would be my first visit to Becky's home in a rural area of Wisconsin. Since I am directionally challenged, even in town, I asked her to send me *detailed* directions because I am apt to get lost on country roads. Her directions were great! I took the correct exit off the interstate, drove a few miles, and turned off on a clearly marked rural road. I was feeling pretty confident that I would arrive at Becky's house without getting lost.

And then it happened! Becky's directions said to go *about* a mile and turn right. But neither of the two roads that were "about a mile" down the road bore a road sign to identify them. And since one was just shy of a mile and the second was just a bit over a mile, I reasoned that either one of them could be the road I wanted.

After trying first one road and then the second road without locating the next landmark on the directions, I gave in and stopped to call Becky. She chuckled as she said, "Oh, yes, I forgot that there is no sign there." She gave me directions to find the road that would lead me to her home. And as I was preparing to hang up the cell phone and get back on the road, she added, "Now you can't miss our home. Chad [her husband] is standing right next to the road, waiting to flag you down." And sure enough, there was Chad, waving and directing me into the driveway.

How grateful I am that the same will be true when I leave this earth. For Jesus has promised that He will be there, waiting to welcome all who believe in Him into the courts of heaven.

I can anticipate this welcome because
I have put my faith in Him.
Can you say the same?

Prayer

Dear Heavenly Father, thank You for sending Your Son to show me the way home to eternity. Strengthen my faith daily so that I may bring others to believe in You too. Amen.

A ROOM WITH
A VIEW, PLEASE

I will lift up mine eyes unto the hills,
from whence cometh my help.

—Psalm 121:1 (KJV)

We were going to vacation in Colorado, the land of snow-capped peaks and rugged foothills. So a top priority, after cleanliness and comfortable beds, was a motel room with a view. As I made the reservations for our five-day stay in various towns, I made this request.

On the day we arrived in Colorado Springs, we drove up to the motel office that was located in one of three buildings on the property. I could hardly wait to get our room assignment so I could fling open the curtains and take in the view. But my hopes were dashed to smithereens when I walked into the room and found myself looking at … the brick wall of the next building. No matter how I tried, there was absolutely no way to see even a tiny speck of the mountains!

I have often been disappointed with my view of life as well. A routine physical turned into a major health challenge. An easy road trip turned into hours of detours and road construction. A promising friendship faded into obscurity. Major personal relationships ended, breaking my heart in the process.

How thankful I am that when I have found myself looking at some of life's highest brick walls, I can still lift my eyes heavenward and know that my help comes from God, who created the earth. I have found that there is no valley in life so deep or brick wall so high that God cannot overcome it. He is there for me, wherever my life's journey has taken me. Because of this, I no longer look at life's brick walls as obstacles that stop me in my tracks but as challenges to be met and overcome with God's help.

For I worship a God who can do anything but still fail.
Have you found this to be true in your life as well?

Prayer

Dear God, with You all things are possible. Thank You for giving me strength to meet the challenges of life. In Jesus' Name I pray. Amen.

HE TOOK MY HAND

For I am the Lord your God who takes hold of your right
hand and says to you, Do not fear; I will help you.

—Isaiah 41:13 (KJV)

She had been my friend for over thirty years. She had congratulated
me in my successes and commiserated with me in my challenges.
She sent a yellow rose when Dad died and brought a casserole
when my son died. And she embraced my ministry as if it were
her own.

And now she lay in her bed under hospice care in her home,
fighting to survive cancer. In the last weeks of her life, I went
there every day. Walking up the sidewalk, I would start to
tremble. What words of comfort did I have for her and for her
precious daughters and her husband? How could I share words
of encouragement with them when I felt so discouraged myself?
How could I put on a happy face when my heart was breaking
with the loss I knew would be coming soon?

Climbing up the porch steps, I knocked on the door while
begging God to go with me and give me the words to say. And,
true to His promise, God took my right hand and guided me
through the time spent with the family. There *were* words to say;
I could share the love of God even in the midst of my pain. And
I could pray a prayer of thankfulness for the life of this lady who
always put others first in her life. She taught me many lessons

through her words and actions. It was a privilege to make those visits for they gave me the opportunity to thank her for the good things she had done for all of us.

But I could not have walked through this valley of sadness if God had not been there to take hold of my right hand and lead me through it.

When is the last time you allowed God to take you by the hand and guide you in life?

Prayer

> Father, You truly blessed me by giving me the gift of friendship with this kind and caring lady. Thank You for holding my hand as together we shared time with her in the final steps of her earthly journey. Amen.

LESS IS MORE

And He said unto them, "Take heed, and beware of covetousness, for a man's life consisteth not in the abundance of the things which he possesseth."

—Luke 12:15 (KJV)

Our family moved many times between my birth and high school graduation. This prompted discarding toys I no longer played with and clothing I had outgrown. But along with these discards, there were also sentimental articles discarded because my parents reasoned that I had "outgrown" them, or they just didn't fit in the box.

Perhaps this explains why I am such a pack rat today. If it weren't for my husband, our attic and basement would be stuffed with magazines I might want to read someday, clothing that might fit after I lose ten (or twenty) pounds, and pieces for craft items I plan to assemble after retirement. I have to admit that I have a very, *very* difficult time giving anything away.

But that is changing. In our thirty years of marriage, I have learned that there is a feeling of freedom that comes with discarding items that no longer fit, are not being used, or may never be read in my lifetime. Surprise and joy flood over me when I discover that I now have room in the attic to hide Christmas presents, and store holiday decorations. And it *is* easier to make wardrobe decisions with all my clothes, both summer and winter, hanging in the same closet; what a concept! I can definitely say with a smile on my face that less stuff has given me more happiness.

I finally believe the age-old concept that less is more.
Is the same true for you?

Prayer

> Thank You, Father, for this great gift of contentment that has come from giving things away and enjoying life more. In Jesus' Name, we pray. Amen.

DAD'S BIBLE

Thy word is a lamp unto my feet, and a light unto my path.

—Isaiah 41:13 (NIV)

My wonderful father has been with the Lord for over ten years. And although I released him willingly into the arms of Jesus when he was ninety-three, there are times when his physical absence eats at my being with the worst kind of emotional pain. He was more than a parent to me; he was a role model, teacher, encourager, and guidance counselor. The years he spent as a pastor in many small American Baptist churches served as years of training for me, setting an example of how to serve as a pastor to a small congregation.

As a role model, his strides of faith gave me a path to follow; his unwavering belief in the Lord set a visible example of discipleship for me to witness and emulate. He was accepting rather than judgmental. He gave to others without thought of receiving back. He forgave, even if it took hours of prayer to attain the ability to release the anger or disappointment he had suffered because of the actions of another person. He owned up to his own mistakes. And even as a child, I knew that Dad's word was his bond; when he made a promise, he kept it.

Perhaps this is why, when I miss Dad the most, when the tears fall unexpectedly, why when my heart hurts the most, the quickest way to connect with both my earthly and heavenly

Fathers is to hold Dad's Bible and read from its precious pages. As I hold Dad's Bible, I can sense the peace that surrounded our family in the days of my youth during morning family devotions. I can once again picture Dad's strong hands holding this precious Holy Book, with its worn black cover and hear the sound of his voice as he read the scriptures and then prayed for each of us.

Today I can truly say that the Word of God does serve as a lamp unto my feet because my Dad taught me that the Holy Word of God is the best map for life.

Will our family members remember when our hands held God's precious Word?

Prayer

> Thank You, God, for a father who took the time daily to instruct me in Your Word. Amen.

SAY THANKS ... TODAY

The desire of a man is his kindness.

—Proverbs 19:22 (KJV)

For the past few years, a salesman named Mike had waited on me during the majority of my monthly visits to the local Sears store. Mike was always welcoming, friendly, courteous, and efficient. Because of his big smile, pleasant disposition, and helpful attitude, I felt like a valued customer, even though I was there only to make a payment. Sadly, I never took the opportunity to thank Mike for the great service I always received. I never once told him how much his positive attitude and pleasant disposition meant to me.

Now it's too late for I learned just a few days ago that the reason I hadn't seen him during the last few months wasn't because he was busy in the stockroom or had a day off. It was because Mike's valiant battle with cancer was ending. (I never even knew he was ill.) And even though we had been praying for Mike through our church because his aunt, a church member, had put him on the list of prayer concerns, I didn't know that the Mike on our prayer list was Mike from the Sears store because I never knew his last name.

I went to Mike's memorial service and sat in the chapel, where every seat was filled. I pondered the number of people who had come to pay their respects and wondered if some of them also wished for one more opportunity to speak with Mike. And while

I will never be able to thank Mike for the special imprint he left on my life, I can pass his kindness on to others. I can say thanks to other clerks, waitresses, and people who, like Mike, go the extra mile to provide great customer service.

May the spirit of Mike live on in my life—and yours—
as we thank those who do a great job!

Prayer

Dear God, You have taught us to give thanks in all things. Prod me to take the time to be thankful to all who do a good job. In Jesus' Name we pray. Amen.

NOT EVEN A TINY *WOOF*

Time to keep silence, and a time to speak.

—Ecclesiastes 3:7 (KJV)

There she sat in the corner kennel at the dog pound, a nine-pound ball of silky fur with dark eyes and a moist pink nose. While all around her, eleven large dogs were barking at full volume, she sat looking straight ahead, never uttering even so much as a tiny *Woof.* She was doing her best to ignore the noise and mass confusion around her, but one could see that this trembling little Poodle-Maltese puppy was very unhappy. I glanced at her, but kept walking because my husband had indicated that he wanted a larger dog. As I rounded the corner to walk down the next aisle, I heard his voice from three steps behind me asking, "What do you think about this one?"

I turned to see him looking at the beautiful little dog, and my heart was filled with joy for she was just what I had hoped for. She became our beloved little Cookie, and we never regretted our decision to adopt her.

I often think of that day in the kennel and how Cookie won our hearts without barking once or even looking in our direction. And I realize that the messages of fear and need of comfort she transmitted with her actions were much more powerful than any bark she could have sent in our direction.

Perhaps I need to follow Cookie's example and talk less. For while I can speak for hours about how much God loves us, sometimes too many words can get in the way and turn people away from the good news of the Gospel. Many people are tired of hearing about the difference God makes in our lives; they need to see God's love demonstrated in actions of kindness, forgiveness, and compassion, actions that do speak in a much more powerful way.

So it is true, actions do speak much louder than words, especially in our spiritual lives.

Prayer

Dear Father, help me to show others today, and every day, that having You in my life does make a difference. In Jesus' Name I pray. Amen.

A LETTER FROM GRANDMA

Paul, an apostle of Jesus Christ by the will of God, and Timothy
our brother, unto the church of God which is at Corinth.

—2 Corinthians 1:1 (KJV)

I think the apostle Paul was on to something when he wrote the
letters to the early churches that comprise the majority of the
New Testament. For Paul's letters were treasured and cherished
as tangible reminders of his love and respect for those in the
congregations. Oh, yes, some of Paul's letters were filled with
reprimands and criticism; Paul felt it was his duty to advise the
churches on following the teachings of Jesus. But even as Paul
disciplined the church members, his words revealed his deep-
seated concern and love for the mission of the church and its
members.

Letter-writing today is almost a lost art. And this is sad. I
remember the joy I felt as a child when we would receive a letter
from Grandma Krell. Written on blue-lined paper in her left-
handed style, Dad would often have to stop and decipher a word
here and there. But it was worth it for she related stories from
her daily life working in the button factory in Muscatine, Iowa,
and a story or two from Grandpa's days as an elementary school
janitor. And when Dad got down to the final paragraph, Grandma

always named each one of us and told us how much she loved us. Even now, over fifty years later, remembering her letters makes me feel loved.

So perhaps the apostle Paul, and my Grandma Krell were on to something. Their letters made a difference. I think it's time I follow their example and write some letters. With friends in six or seven states whom I haven't talked to in ages, we do have a lot to catch up on.

What better way is there to say, "I care,"
than to sit down and write a letter?

Prayer

Dear God, thank You for the ability to write. Help me to take the opportunity to reach out to the special people in my life and say thank you for the friendship we share. This I pray in Jesus' Name. Amen.

IS RETIREMENT
A SEASON?

To everything there is a season, and a time
to every purpose under the heaven.

—Ecclesiastes 3:1 (KJV)

Fourteen years ago, I found myself standing on the edge of a couple of "seasons" in my life. And even though the writer of Ecclesiastes never came right out and said so, there does seem to be a time in life to retire and move on.

For me, that time was August 2006. After eighteen years, I was leaving a position in a local vending company that had challenged me professionally while affording me the opportunity to make some new and lasting friends. The decision to leave did not come easily, but the lure of more free time to write, fish, and spend time with my husband overrode the qualms I had about leaving the office I had come to regard as my second home. And it should be noted here that, while I left this full-time position, I continued to serve as a part-time pastor to a small congregation, so it wasn't full-time retirement.

In facing the future with its great unknowns in the first months after retirement, I became much closer to God. When the first Friday came and I didn't receive a paycheck—and then more Fridays without paychecks—I must admit that I felt pangs of panic. Would my Social Security and part-time pay from the church be enough to cover expenses? When I would encounter a former coworker at the supermarket who shared news of other coworkers, I would feel a momentary ache at not being included in what was going in the workplace. And yet, even as I experienced these emotions, I was learning that there is no "season" that I move into that God is not already there.

It has taken a while for me to settle into the new rhythm of having only one job. It has been a major adjustment to have free time to go places and do things in the daytime. At first I felt guilty for I had never, in all my adult years, had such freedom. But through all the adjustments in the new season of retirement, God has remained a constant presence who continues to guide me into new and exciting places and friendship.

New seasons bring new challenges.
Thankfully, God is always there to help us meet them.

Prayer

Thank You, God, for each new season. May I embrace it as a true gift from You. Amen.

A FAILURE IN MATH

Old things are passed away; behold, all things are become new.
—2 Corinthians 5:17 (KJV)

During my eighth-grade year, I was given an aptitude test to determine if I should be placed in general math or algebra as a freshman. I must have been at the top of my game on test day because I somehow passed the test with flying colors. But it didn't take me long as a high-school freshmen to realize that I was way out of my league in algebra. I didn't understand it from day 1 and received a near-failing grade on my report card, a first for me. My dad, a math major in college, nearly went into orbit when he saw that grade. He let me know in no uncertain terms that, working together, that grade was going to be higher at the end of the next semester.

But Dad hadn't figured on the "new math" that was being taught in our high school. It was much different than what he had learned, and it took him some time to figure how the new math system worked. In the meantime, he taught me the "old way" to do algebra, and miracles of miracles, I could arrive at the right answer in less than one class period.

In today's world there seems to be a lot of "new" religion being taught. This involves taking shortcuts through scripture, skipping over parts determined to be irrelevant, and taking other verses out of context to prove that what we are doing is okay.

The problem with the so-called new religion is that God wrote the Book, and He knows what it says. And when we stand before Him on judgment day, He won't be grading on the curve. So I think I'll just stick to the "old-time religion" and keep reading the lessons that God wrote down for me to learn.

For if the old time religion was good enough for Dad and Mom, then it's good enough for me.

Prayer

> Remind me, Dear Father, that "new and improved" isn't always the best. Prod me to stick to the basics when it comes to Your lessons for my life. In Jesus' Name I pray. Amen.

VIOLETS THAT BLOOM?

Thou visitest the earth, and watereth it.

—Psalm 65:9 (KJV)

Like my mother before me, I grow violets, although not nearly as successfully as she did. While most of her plants nearly always had blooms on them, I feel fortunate if two out of the five I own are in bloom at the same time. In fact, I often think that growing violets is one way God keeps me humble for I can never brag on my success.

But all is not lost for my violets have taught me some valuable lessons. If they don't get sun in an east window (at least at my home), they will grow leaves but very few blooms, teaching me that if I don't get enough light from Jesus, the Light of the World, every day, I will go right on living … but not too successfully.

Violets need to be planted in pots with openings at the bottom and set in saucers. Water is poured into the saucers, and the violets soak it up into the roots through the pot openings. In my life, I too "soak up" what is going on around me. If the atmosphere is full of doubt and fear, I become doubtful and fearful. If negativity surrounds me, I develop a negative attitude. But if I associate with positive individuals who have goals set in life, have their eyes on Jesus, and have placed their faith in Him, I become energized and full of life. I soak up their energy and their attitudes and live life in a positive manner.

My outlook on life is determined by the personalities and energies I "soak up" from those around me.

Prayer

Thank You, Father, for friends who support me in my faith and energize me with their witnessing. May I learn from them, and go forth to serve You better. In Jesus' Name, Amen.

SERIOUSLY? STAY CALM?

In quietness and in confidence shall be your strength.
—Isaiah 30:15 (KJV)

"Be calm and trust You?" I inwardly raged as I finished reading my morning devotions. "Be calm? In this workplace, God? There are so many raw emotions just waiting to boil over. Signs of stress and anxiety are evident in every department; harsh words and outbursts of anger are exchanged on a regular basis. Everyone is seriously overworked and underpaid. When employees leave for other jobs, they are not replaced, creating more work for those left behind. Promised cost-of-living raises fail to materialize, driving blood pressures to new highs and creating more anxiety as employees struggle to keep their bills paid and their families fed.

"How can I be quiet? Be confident? Be calm? Even if I *could* stay calm behind the closed door of my office, it is all blown away when I have to leave my desk and start down the hall. I only have to meet one stressed person who has reached his or her boiling point, and my peace is shattered. Be calm? How do I do that?"

And then I recall the story of that tiny little boat on the Sea of Galilee, the boat that held frantic disciples who battled the storm while Jesus lay sleeping in the bow. I feel sure that nerves were jangling, voices were raised, and blood pressures soared then too. And I recall that it was only when the disciples reached out to Jesus that He brought peace in the storm.

As one of His modern-day disciples, I too need to reach out to Him amid the storms of my life. Only then will I find the peace that He has promised to all who believe in Him.

> Amid the storms of life, join me in reaching
> out to the One who calmed the storm.

Prayer

> Dear God, help me to reach out in the midst of the winds of the workplace to claim the peace that only can come from You. Amen.

I'LL BAKE THE BREAD

Knead it, and make cakes upon the hearth.

—Genesis 18:6 (KJV)

On the morning of my first Monday as a housemother in the Kodiak Baptist Children's Home, the relief housemother named Mildred asked if I would like to bake bread or do the laundry. Since I had taught myself to bake bread as a newlywed and could turn out two loaves quite nicely, I volunteered to bake. Little did I know just how big the job was!

Mildred went into the pantry and returned with the largest bag of flour I had ever seen, a huge metal bowl, a stack of twelve bread pans, and a quart jar full of yeast. "Here is the recipe," she said with a smile on her face. "This should get you started. I think you know where everything else is." And with that, Mildred turned on her heel and retreated to the laundry room in the basement.

Later that day—at 4:50 p.m. to be exact—there were twelve loaves of bread sitting on the counter, waiting to be eaten in the next two days by fourteen hungry children. And me? I was exhausted from the kneading and the pounding that went into making all that bread.

I learned an unforgettable lesson that day. Like bread dough, I often get puffed up with my own sense of importance and self-worth. And it is then that God "kneads" the dough of my life to once again give me room to grow in faith and humility. The Bible teaches that "pride goeth before destruction and a haughty spirit before a fall" (Proverbs 16:18 KJV). And when my life is full of pride, the yeast of faith has no room to grow.

Humility is a virtue. May I continually seek to be humble.

Prayer

> Help me, Father, to allow Your Word to be the yeast that fills my life with fullness. Amen.

STEPPING-STONES

One thing have I desired of the Lord ... that I may
dwell in the house of the Lord all the days of my life.
—Psalm 27:4 (KJV)

During four decades in life, I held a wide variety of office positions. Starting as a file clerk, I slowly advanced up through the ranks to achieve the position of office manager. With each new job, I gained skills in accounting, data entry, and personnel management.

Today I am a pastor. And as I look back over my career in business, I realize that I was a "pastor-in-training" on those earlier jobs. The experience I gained while sitting behind the desks of several businesses is proving invaluable in serving God in the church setting.

Even though I was unaware of it, God was laying out the stepping-stones toward the pulpit as I worked as a receptionist, office manager, public relations representative, executive administrator, and data processor. As I moved upward on my career paths through each of these positions, I had no idea what my final career destination would be. However, I did know Who my guide was for I had put my faith and my future in God's hands. Today I am thrilled that God's stepping-stones have led me to work in the place I most love to be, and that is in the house of the Lord.

Can you look back and see the stepping-stones God laid out for your life?

Prayer

Thank You, God, for walking with me through the days of my life. May I always treasure each day in Your house and in Your service. Amen.

READ THE PSALMS

My flesh and my heart faileth, but God is the
strength of my heart and my portion forever.

—Psalm 73:26 (KJV)

Dad's ninety-three-year journey through life was nearing an
end. And as I sped through the darkness of night on my three-
hundred-mile journey north to reach his bedside, my cell phone
rang at 2 a.m. Pulling over to the shoulder, I answered a call from
Pastor Dave, telling me that due to his own failing health, he was
going to have to leave Dad's bedside to return home.

"I certainly understand, Pastor Dave," I responded. "I'll be
there in another hour or so. Just tell me how Dad is doing."

"Basically he is being kept comfortable by the Hospice team.
Occasionally he becomes quite agitated, however. When he does,
just read him some verses from the Psalms. That quiets him very
quickly."

Many times in the hours between my arrival and Dad's
departure for eternity, I followed Pastor Dave's advice. And in
those final hours, I witnessed how my Dad, who had preached
the Gospel for over sixty years, indeed found peace in the words
of the shepherd boy, David, as he moved through the valley of
the shadow of death and into the presence of God. I am grateful
for Dad's pastor, who took the time to pass on the wisdom that
aided me in sharing in this one last spiritual journey with Dad.

Will you join me in giving thanks for pastors
who guide us in difficult times?

Prayer

Dear God, give me wisdom to cling to the
scriptures in all the days of my life that I may
find comfort both in living and in dying. In Jesus'
Name, I pray. Amen.

TAKE OUR BENCH

Stand up in the presence of the elderly,
and show respect for the aged.
—Leviticus 19:32 (TLB)

I had walked around the festival for almost forty-five minutes, and now I needed a place to sit and rest. But the only bench in sight was occupied by two young girls in their teens who laughed as they played with their phones. Standing across the narrow hall, I wondered if perhaps there was room for me on that bench too. But the thought was fleeting as I could see that there wasn't room for one more person.

Just then one of the girls looked up from her phone and spotted me standing alone in the hallway. Hesitating just a moment, she stood up and said, "Here, you can have our bench. We should get going to meet our parents."

Thanking her for her kindness, I sank down on the bench to rest my weary back and legs, silently thanking God for the young girl who sensed my need and offered me her seat. And even as I whispered this prayer, I resolved to keep my eyes open for others in need as well, for the girl's actions reminded me that ...

Small deeds of kindness do make a big
difference in the lives of others.

Prayer

Dear Father, too often our youth get a bad rap in today's world. Help me begin to change that by speaking good about them at every opportunity. Thanks, God, for hearing my prayer. In Jesus' Name I pray. Amen.

ROAD RAGE

And give thee peace.

—Numbers 6:26 (KJV)

It was a classic case of road rage. But it didn't happen on a road; it happened in the parking lot of a local convenience store.

While on my way to a city park, I decided to stop and get a soft drink. Signaling my intention to turn, I drove into the parking lot and prepared to turn right, into the end space. But a sudden movement to my left caused me to slam on the brakes. It seems that the drover approaching me wanted that parking space too. Literally driving in front of me, he made a left turn and took the end parking space! As I sat there with my foot still jammed on the brake, he got out of his car, turned to me, and yelled, "Watch where you're going, lady. You're not the only driver on the road!"

"But I was there first!" I countered.

Walking around my car, he leaned down and pushed his face in through the open window of my Honda Civic. "Well just how was I to know where you wanted to park? Yours is not the only car on the road!" He then turned on his heel and strode into the store.

And what did I do after I finished parking my car? When I stopped shaking, I prayed! I closed my eyes and thanked God for protecting me. I then asked God to watch over this man and allow him—and everyone else driving near him—to arrive safely at their destinations.

And the soft drink I had stopped to purchase? I went to the park without it.

> Instead of losing our tempers with angry motorists,
> let us pray for them instead.

Prayer

> Dear Heavenly Father, be with those who are angry and frustrated today. Give them the peace that can come only from You. Amen.

I AM BLESSED

There shall be showers of blessing.

—Ezekiel 34:26 (KJV)

Immediately following my retirement from my clerical position, my husband and I went on an extended vacation out West. Thinking back to the many places and adventures we encountered, I realize how many blessings I have taken for granted.

As I think about Trail Town in Cody, Wyoming, with its primitive prairie homes, schools, and stores, I give thanks for the modern conveniences of furnaces, electricity, and indoor plumbing. The sudden illness in Jackson Hole, Wyoming, gives me reason to be thankful for doctors, nurses, and nearby drugstores. Seeing buffalo up close and personal right outside the car window, and remembering how they once were a primary source of food, I give thanks for modern-day markets, where food and produce are readily available. Panning for gold in a cold California stream (and yes, finding just a little bit) prods me to give thanks for a steadier—and warmer—way to earn a living. And standing in the yard of a ranch once owned by someone I deeply admired reminds me to give thanks for the mentors and role models who have assisted me in setting personal and spiritual life goals.

The memories of this trip have illuminated a host of blessings to be thankful for. But perhaps the two blessings that are etched most deeply upon my heart are these: In every town and restaurant we went into, we were total strangers. No one knew our names; we were two people alone in a sea of faces. Out of this came great gratitude for the people I am privileged to call my friends, people who not only know my name but also are there for me on both the happy and sad days of my life. And the second blessing? Having a warm, safe home to return to,

Let's count blessings every day, not just on Thanksgiving day!

Prayer

> Thank You, God, for Your showers of blessing.
> May I treasure them as true gifts from You. Amen.

A RODEO IN CODY

You have let me experience the joys of life.

—Psalm 96:11

I saw my first rodeo in Ft. Dodge, Iowa, in 1962; I was hooked for life. Watching the pageantry of the opening ceremony followed by the contests between cowboys and beasts rekindled an earlier interest in the Old West. The sheer heroics of the cowboys, paired with the hard and precise work of the horses, gave me a new insight of what running a ranch must entail.

In the many years since that first rodeo, I have taken every opportunity to attend others and was thrilled to learn that there is a yearly one held in Ft. Madison, which is just twenty miles down the road from home. But none of these rodeos had begun to prepare me for a night in Cody, Wyoming, that I will never forget.

Driving into Cody that morning, we were awestruck by the rugged beauty of the mountains around us. It was so unlike our scenery back home in Iowa that every new vista challenged us to totally appreciate the beauty we were seeing.

Arriving at the hotel, we hurriedly checked in and carried our bags up to the room, excited that we had indeed been given a room with a view that we had requested. Rushing back to the car, we drove downtown to look for the famed Irma Hotel, where Wild Bill Cody stayed when he was in town. After locating and exploring it, we began to walk the surrounding streets, mingling with other tourists as we gawked into store windows. And that's when I saw the sign: "RODEO TONIGHT."

"Can we go?" I fairly shrieked to my husband. "It would be great to see a real live authentic western rodeo in Cody, Wyoming. It just couldn't get any better than this! Can we go?"

Not a rodeo fan himself but knowing how much this meant to me, he said, "Yes, we can go." Hours later we sat in the stands and watched as the setting sun gave way to a full moon while cool September breezes ruffled the flags in the arena. I sat in awe as event after event unfolded before us, bringing to fulfillment one of my youthful dreams of seeing a rodeo "out west," where it all began. And as I walked out of the arena, I was reminded that God's blessings often come when we least expect them and in the most unexpected places.

The time to recognize and give thanks
for unexpected blessings is now.
Will you join me?

Prayer

Thank You, Father, for allowing me to experience
this great joy in my life.

Amen.

WORRY LESS, PRAY MORE

Take therefore no thought for the morrow: for the
morrow shall take thought for the things of itself.
—Matthew 6:34 (KJV)

I inwardly groaned when my physician set up an appointment
for a bone density test. "You are at the age now where this test
is much more important," the doctor said. And thus, on the
appointed day, I went into the clinic for the test. I was surprised
at how easily it was completed, and how quickly. What I wasn't
prepared for was the dread that seemed to envelop me as I left
the clinic. *What if it shows that my bones are weakening? Or what if
I am growing shorter, like Mom did? What if I'm not as healthy as I
think I am? What if I have to start taking medicine that costs a fortune?*
I wondered.

As I got into the car and drove away, my positive attitude
about life evaporated, and negative thoughts replaced it. And
throughout the day, the darkness of negativity hung over me like
a dark storm cloud.

At 4:30 that afternoon, I was sitting in my office, attempting
to write next Sunday's sermon when my husband called to say
that I was to call the doctor's office right away. I thought, *Here it
comes! Something is wrong!*

Dialing the number, I whispered a silent prayer for strength to
accept whatever the results would indicate. Imagine my shock and

surprise when the nurse reported that the results were the same as the test taken three years earlier. My bones were still strong, and my height remained the same.

I received great news that day, news that humbled me when I realized that not once that day had I prayed about the results. Instead…I had worried about them.

> When was the last time you and I worried
> when we should have been praying?

Prayer

> Father, You teach me in Your Holy Word to avoid worrying about tomorrow. Help me learn that lesson to avoid more stress in the future. In Jesus' Name I pray. Amen.

NEVER ALONE

Lord, do You remember that time when my
heart was so filled with turmoil?

—Psalm 131:1 (TLB)

While sitting on my worn brown couch to begin my morning devotions, I was totally unprepared to answer the above question. For in asking God that question, I was prompted to remember those difficult, turmoil-filled times as well. Unheeded, the memories of the days following the unexpected death of my son whirled into my consciousness at the speed of lightning. The word "turmoil" doesn't even begin to describe the hopelessness and helplessness I felt in the dark days after I learned of his death.

Another time of turmoil came when the truck repair business I had worked in as office manager for eight years closed down with little warning, leaving me without a job. How would I support my son and myself without an income? What was I going to do?

And then there was the painful decision to resign as our church's Director of Christian Education after almost seven fun-filled years. It was not a decision made lightly but came only after hours of prayer, and which resulted in my stepping into the field of pulpit supply and ultimately into the field of ministry.

Oh, yes, my mind called up many times of turmoil over broken bones and illnesses that prevented my going to work.

Times of uncertainty as my sons began to find their niches in the great game of life, times of low self-esteem and feelings of hopelessness as I struggled through some of life's biggest storms.

Many came as a result of poor choices and decisions. Others were the result of unexpected circumstances and difficulties. But through each and every one of them, from the biggest to the tiniest, I have never, ever, been alone. Even when I failed to look up to God for the strength and wisdom to weather these times of turmoil, He was always there waiting. He was just a prayer away.

Today I am thankful that I worship a God who never leaves or forsakes me. To God be the glory.

Will you join me in thanking God for His
never-ending presence and love?

Prayer

Dear Father, open the eyes of my heart and my soul to Your ever-present presence. Give me strength as I move through the times of turmoil. In Jesus' Name I pray. Amen.

HICCUPS

Rejoicing in hope, patient in tribulation,
continuing instant in prayer.

—Romans 12:12 (KJV)

I had finished my early morning devotions and was preparing to pray when I got the hiccups. At first I found it rather amusing for I rarely, if ever, got the hiccups. But then things began to turn serious.

I tried holding my breath while counting to ten; that didn't help. I went into the kitchen and drank a glass of ice water; that didn't help. I walked around for several minutes while trying to think calming thoughts, all the while hoping the hiccups would subside on their own; they didn't!

"Why now, God?" I fretted. "I got up early to spend extra time reading Your Holy Word and the devotional that went with it. I spent time thinking about how today's Scripture fit into my life. Now it's time to pray. But I'm all agitated and can't think straight. I just can't pray when I've got the hiccups, God!"

Or could I? Nowhere in the Bible do I find a verse that instructs me to pray only when the conditions are ideal and I am perfectly calm. God doesn't want me to wait for perfect conditions to pray. He wants me to pray at all times and for all things in my life. He is always waiting to hear from me day and night, and yes, even on weekends and when I have the hiccups.

I must learn to pray in spite of adverse conditions. For spending time with God helps smooth out the hiccups of life, whatever they may be.

Do you think you could pray when you had the hiccups?

Prayer

> Dear Father, thank You for being there at all times to hear my prayers. Help me to be as willing to pray as You are to listen. This I pray in Jesus' Name. Amen.

I CAN PRAY

Who giveth rain upon the earth, and
sendeth water upon the fields.

—Job 5:10 (KJV)

It was 9:00 p.m., and the fierce storm that had blown into Green Lake, Wisconsin, had worn itself out. The rain had beat against the windows of the Inn where I was staying, and the lightning bolts had lit up my room. And now it was quiet. But I wasn't. I was restless. I had tarried over dessert earlier in the evening as my dearest friend told me of the health challenges her husband was facing. And it tore at my heart that this woman, who devoted so much of her life to God and to working as His disciple in serving others—including me during the darkest chapters of my life—was now being called to be the home health-care provider for her husband. With her own challenges with heart issues, could she care for her husband around the clock and stay healthy herself?

Struggling with these thoughts prevented me from settling down for the night. Finally, in desperation, I decided to go for a walk in the cool night air to clear my mind.

And as I walked the familiar path past the Vesper Circle, where I had gone to pray so many times in earlier years, I was reminded that I could do very little to ease my friend's concern. But the God Whom I believe and trust in can and will be with my friend every step of the way. And the best way I can assist her in the difficult journey ahead is to continually lift her up to God in prayer, just as she has done for me in the many years we have been friends.

Together, let us resolve to pray daily for special friends in need.

Prayer

> Thank You, God, for the gift of friendship and for this lady who has graced my life with her friendship. Be with her as she cares for her husband. This I ask in the Name of Jesus. Amen.

RAYS OF LOVE

Let him who walks in the dark who has no light trust
in the name of the Lord, and rely on his God.
—Isaiah 50:10 (NIV)

Those first weeks following my son's sudden death were awful.
Not only did I lie for hours staring sleeplessly into space in my
darkened bedroom; I also experienced an inner darkness that
enveloped me even at high noon. It felt like no light could
penetrate my soul. It was as if my world had turned dark and cold.

But my family and friends did their best to filter light into
darkness of my life. A steady stream of sympathy cards arrived
every day, carrying healing words of love and compassion. Each
card brought a glimmer of light from loving individuals who
wanted me to know that they loved me and cared about the pain
I was feeling. And as the cards continued to arrive for weeks after
Ken's death, I began to think of them as rays of God's love, and
the friends who sent them as gifts and precious treasures given to
me by God.

My family and friends never knew how they were used by
God to infiltrate the darkness of my life with the rays of His light
and hope—until now, as they are reading this devotional.

Their kindness and continued efforts in sending cards and
letters demonstrated not only the healing power of friends and
family but also the power of a small greeting card.

Will you join me in sending greeting cards to those who are hurting and alone today?

Prayer

Thank You, God, for the cards that arrived from friends as far away as Kodiak, Alaska, to as near as six blocks across town. Thank You for reminding me, through the thoughtfulness of others, that I wasn't ever alone in my time of darkness. Amen.

WHAT NOW, LORD?

Moses did not know that the skin of his face shown.
—Exodus 34:29 (KJV)

"God, I need You! There is so much to do, and I'm only one person.

There are sick calls to make, a column to write for the church newsletter, a service to conduct at the care facility, and next Sunday's sermon to prepare. And even as I struggle with getting all this done, a church member has just come into my office to grumble about a new element I incorporated into last Sunday's worship service that she didn't like. God, I'm so discouraged right now! I just want to quit for a few days and figure out what to do."

And then I think of poor Moses who was leading all those Israelites to the Promised Land. Talk about grumbling! "Moses, we're hungry!" "Moses, we're thirsty." Moses, take us back to Egypt, We had food to eat there."

Moses heard more grumbling than I will *ever* hear! How did *he* handle it? He stopped and talked to God. Moses asked for guidance, support and direction and God supplied all three.

And now I must do the same. I must ask God to clear my mind and give me direction as I work through the duties before me while soothing the person who is unhappy. And God will guide and support me in my efforts.

When we feel like walking off the spiritual job, it's time to stand still and talk to God.

Prayer

> God, prod me to keep my eyes on You, even as I ask for Your help to continue to move forward in the work You have for me to do. Amen.

I HAVE NOTHING
TO LEAVE YOU

The Lord is the portion of my inheritance.

—Psalm 16:5 (KJV)

Dad has always been my hero. From the time I was four, and he taught me to read, right up until the final years of his life, we could converse on almost any subject with ease. Sometimes the topics were light and humorous; others were difficult and painful. And when emotions ran high and our conversation a little heated, we would agree to put it aside and revisit it at a later time, when we were calmer.

But there was one conversation near the end of his life that upset me far more than he ever knew. After supper one evening, he walked over and sat down heavily in his blue recliner. He seemed agitated, as if he had something to say but wasn't sure how to begin. After some fifteen minutes, Dad looked across the room at me and said, "I am so sorry that I have no inheritance to leave you." His words and the sadness in his voice nearly broke my heart. Struggling to hold back the tears, I told him that I was thankful for the inheritance he had given me and would be eternally grateful for it.

Surprised at my emotional response, he said, "What are you talking about? I haven't given you anything. I have nothing to give. During the years I have served as a pastor, your mother and I always lived in a parsonage, so we never bought a house. I dedicated my life to ministering to small congregations, which didn't pay well, so my finances are limited. So what have I given you as an inheritance?"

Smiling through my tears, I began, "When I was two days old, you adopted me into your family and gave me a home and a name. You taught me how to read, giving me not only a wonderful hobby but enabling me to succeed in my career. You have been a good father, who has stood with me in both the good and the rough times in my life. And you introduced me to Jesus Christ and set an example of how a Christian life should be lived. I am far richer with this inheritance than if you had left me a lot of money, for my faith in Jesus Christ has given me hope for eternity. And Daddy, it just doesn't get any better than that!"

Hearing that, Dad got up out of his chair. He kissed me on the cheek while giving me a goodnight hug and left the room with a smile on his face.

What inheritance will you give God thanks for?

Prayer

> Thank You, God, for the inheritance that my father gave to me.
>
> May I use it, and share it with my children and grandchildren. Amen.

IT'S A NEW DAY

It is of the Lord's mercies that we are not
consumed, because His compassions fail not.

—Lamentations 3:22 (KJV)

I had a morning paper route from sixth grade through high school, which meant that I often left the house while the earth was still cloaked in total darkness. Riding along with sixty papers stuffed in my bicycle basket, the only sounds would be the occasional hum of a passing car or the thud of the paper as it hit the porch I threw it on.

But after delivering the first ten or twelve papers, I would hear the song of a single bird … then two birds … and then even more, until it seemed that all the trees I pedaled under were filled with birds warming up for the arrival of dawn. As the sun appeared and the air warmed up, I was not only bathed in bright sunlight but also serenaded by hundreds of birds singing in concert to greet the new day.

As a young girl, I didn't fully appreciate the experience of the dawning of a new day for I was too engrossed in getting the papers delivered on time and riding back home for breakfast.

But my appreciation has grown over the years. And now, on those mornings when it is warm enough to sit on my front porch in the predawn darkness, I savor those moments when the first bird sings, accompanied very shortly by its other feathered friends.

And it is then that I give thanks for the loving kindness of my heavenly Father that begins afresh every day. What a joy it is to experience not only the song of the birds and the warmth of the sun, but also to begin every day anew in God's love and kindness. It truly makes every day special!

Together let us greet each new day with thanksgiving!

Prayer

> Dear Father, although I am no longer outside at dawn, remind me with the rays of morning sunlight and the sound of singing birds that You have blessed me with another day. Then prod me to use each hour to glorify Your name. Amen.

I FELT TRAPPED

Let words of my mouth and the meditation
of my heart be acceptable in Thy sight, O
Lord, my Strength and my Redeemer.

—Psalm 19:14 (KJV)

It was near the end of the monthly luncheon at the neighborhood diner. The fourteen of us gathered around the tables had been brought up to date on the news from family and friends as we enjoyed the food set before us. Everyone was in a good mood as they listened to the conversations going on around them. But then all that changed near the end of the meal.

Four or five ladies at the far end of the table began discussing a movie they had seen the previous weekend. The content of the movie, and their remarks about some of the scenes in it, were very offensive and in my opinion, bordered on obscenity. Of course the women didn't mean for everyone to hear what they were saying. But as they began to interrupt and talk over each other in their rush to express their opinions, their voices carried easily in the small room.

A lady sitting near me, knowing I am a pastor, leaned over and whispered, "Aren't you going to do something to stop these remarks? They shouldn't be talking like that."

I felt trapped.

How would you have felt? What action would you have taken? Would you have become the "conscience" of the group by standing and asking those making the offensive remarks to change the subject?

I have to admit that I took no action other than to pick up my bill and depart. After stopping to pay at the cash register, I retreated to the car to begin the trip home. As I struggled with what I had (and hadn't) done, all I could think was, *What would Jesus have done?*

What would you have done?

Prayer

> Dear Father, forgive me when I falter in my witness for You. Give me courage to live my faith in difficult situations so that Your name will be glorified. Thank You, Father. Amen.

SQUARES ON A CALENDAR

Whether we live therefore, or die, we are the Lord's.

—Romans 14:8 (KJV)

"For goodness sake," I tell myself, "they are just tiny numbered squares on a piece of paper with the word 'November' at the top of the page." And yet as I glance at the squares bearing the numbers 9 (Dad's birthday), 12 (my parents' anniversary), 20 (the birthday of a very special person), and 24 (the day my son died), I am filled with overwhelming sadness and pain. It's not that I want to experience again the sadness that came with losing these precious loved ones. The sadness comes on its own, unbidden.

It has taken a lot of prayer to diminish the pain as I turn the calendar each year from October to November. And yet I know beyond all doubt that the Lord knows the emotions that well up inside me when turning that calendar page. That is why each year at that moment, He pours an extra measure of strength and endurance out for me. He has already walked with me through the valley of the shadow of death, and now, each year, He is restoring my soul and leading me forth to enjoy the still waters.

Perhaps in a few years I will be able to give thanks for every day of the month of November with good thoughts and a slight smile. For each of the individuals mentioned touched my life and made it better, leaving me with many good memories. And for that, I give thanks.

Difficult month in your life?
Give it to God, and allow Him to walk
through the days with you.

Prayer

Dear Father, instead of bemoaning the feelings of loss as I look at those tiny numbered squares, prod me to give thanks for the years I shared with those individuals. Help me turn weeping into laughter as I remember shared experiences with them. This I pray in Jesus' Name. Amen.

STILL A CHILD AT HEART

Lo, children are an heritage of the Lord.
—Psalm 127:3 (KJV)

He was very young when I began teaching him to read. Little did I know that one day he would far outshine me…..for he is a high achiever.

Today, in his fifties, he has written and published books, earned many awards, has a good standing in the academic community, and is constantly bettering himself as a person and as a leader.

And yet when he comes home to visit, he is, in many ways, still the child I taught to read so many years ago. He loves to eat chocolate chip cookies, explore new ideas, and look at photographs. Sleeping late is still a habit, as is leaving his bed unmade unless prompted to do otherwise.

The child who has grown into a man is still a child at heart … my child. And I hope he realizes that he never has to earn my love or respect for I love him just because he is my child.

I give thanks that the same holds true of my heavenly Father. He sees the "unmade beds" of neglect in my life, and He sees how I often "stay sleeping" when there are tasks to accomplish for Him. And yet He still loves me and forgives me because I am His child.

Together let us thank God for loving us as His children.

Prayer

> Dear Father, thank You for seeing the child in me and still loving me unconditionally. Teach me to treat others as I want to be treated, and to see others as my brothers and sisters in Your family. This I pray in Jesus' Name. Amen.

MUSHROOMS
EVERYWHERE

And the eyes of the blind shall see.

—Isaiah 29:18 (KJV)

It was the second time my husband and I went mushroom hunting, and it wasn't going well for me. Although he had shown great patience in teaching me how to spot mushrooms, my almost-empty bag was still hanging limply upon my arm.

With only a few minutes left before time to head home, he called me over and said, "It's been a long day and a long hike in here. You must be exhausted. So why don't you just stay here and look around while I check out one more section of the woods? There's no sense in both of us tromping around in there! Just hang out here, and I'll be back shortly."

As I watched him disappear into the woods, I wondered why I couldn't see the mushrooms. I knew they were there because his bag was almost full—quite a contrast to the handful in my bag. *Oh, well, no use wandering around! I've let him down! I know that he had such high hopes that this would be something we could do together every spring, but I just can't seem to spot them. Heaven knows, I've been trying.*

Holding my own little pity-party, I stood with slumped shoulders and head down, halfway glancing at the area around me. And then I spotted it … a mushroom. Or was it? Fearing it was a figment of my imagination, I practically tiptoed over to bend down to pick it. And as I did, I spotted another mushroom less than a foot away. And then another. And another.

I couldn't believe my luck! There were lots of mushrooms, all together on the edge of this field, and I was standing right in the middle of them.

Little did I know that my husband had found this patch earlier and had carefully positioned me so that I would be the one to "find" and pick them.

When he heard my shouts of joy, he sauntered casually out of the woods and asked, "What's going on?" It wasn't until several weeks later that he confessed his plan to help me find mushrooms. What a guy!

> When is the last time you found yourself standing
> in the middle of a field of blessings?

Prayer

> Thank You, God, for the love and understanding
> of this man I call my husband. And thank You
> for the blessings You surround me with each day.
> This I pray in the Name of Jesus. Amen

THE MOST IMPORTANT
BOOK OF ALL

Bring the cloak that I left with Carpus … and the books.

—2 Timothy 4:13 (NKJV)

For over fifteen years, I had ten books that I reread every year without fail. Among them were: *A Touch of Wonder* (Arthur Gordon), *The Power of Positive Thinking* (Norman Vincent Peale), *To Kill a Mockingbird* (Harper Lee), *Shepherd of the Hills* (Harold Bell Wright), a book of prayers called *Bless This Mess* (Jo Carr and Imogene Sorley), and *What Happens When Women Pray* (Evelyn Christensen). These books literally had hundreds of miles on them for I packed them into the trunk of my motorcycle or the back seat of my car to read a few pages whenever time allowed. Some copies became so travel-weary that I held them together with a rubber band until I could afford to replace them.

Friends asked why I read the same books every year, to which I replied, "I discover something new each time I read them. They also remind me that even a lesson well-learned can be forgotten if not called to memory on a regular basis."

The same applies to my reading of the Holy Scriptures. I need to reexperience the "path beside still waters" described in the Twenty-third Psalm and be reminded that "I can do all things through Christ, which strengthens me" (Philippians 4:13 NKJV).

Getting caught up once again in the joy of that first Christmas Eve and the excitement of Easter morning in the garden reenergizes me when my spirits get low. Standing with Mary and Martha outside the tomb of their brother Lazarus reminds me that God can create miracles in the most unlikely situations. Even as I read the story of what happens when women pray in one accord, I need to stand once again with the disciples and say, "Lord, teach us to pray" (Luke 11:1 KJV).

All ten of the books on the "required reading" list still sit on my bookshelves to be picked up and read from time to time. But the Book that lies within easy reach for regular reading is God's Holy Word, the Bible. There is always a new lesson to be learned and a message to remember. From the prophesies of Isaiah to the strong words of Paul, God continually teaches me new lessons and disciplines me in my weaknesses. The Bible is the inspired Word of God, a never-ending fountain of knowledge.

> Let us together give thanks for the freedom
> to own and read God's Holy Word.

Prayer

> Dear Father, teach me to use Your Word as a, "lamp unto my feet and a light unto my path" (Psalm 119:105). Amen.

I PALED IN COMPARISON

Neglect not the gift that is in thee.

—1 Timothy 4:14 (KJV)

I have often fallen into the trap of comparing myself with others. "Why can't I be as outgoing as Sandy? Why can't I have a sense of fashion like Betty? Why can't I develop more compassion like Carol? Will I ever be able to cook as well as Debbie or Janet?"

Every time I fall into this trap, I make myself feel inadequate, and miserable. Instead of looking up and thanking God for the strengths in my life, I look down at myself and consider only the weaknesses. This is totally unacceptable and calls for a change.

So I'm going to thank God for the violets blooming on my windowsill, knowing that not everyone can grow violets. I'm going to delight in the ability of playing the piano, aware that I wouldn't trade this ability for that of planning the perfect wardrobe. When I am privileged to spend time with a senior in his or her home, I will thank God that this doesn't require an outgoing personality but instead a caring heart.

Starting today, I am going to quit comparing myself with others and instead thank God for the gifts and talents that I am blessed with. For these qualities can be used to make other lives better if I start looking up and praising God.

Every day, together, let us be thankful and
fully use our God-given talents!

Prayer

Dear Father in heaven, even as I admire the
strengths of others, help me to recognize the
strengths You have blessed me with. May I use
them to glorify Your Name each and every day.
Amen.

MORE LIKE MARY

Who can find a virtuous woman? For
her price is far above rubies.

—Proverbs 31:10 (KJV)

Today, as I write this, I am weary. I have said my earthly farewells
to a dear friend named Mary, who challenged me to become the
best that I could be. Mary was the one who encouraged me to
step out of my comfort zone and attempt new things with and for
God. Mary was the one who consoled me when my attempts and
plans didn't always work out the way I wanted them to.

Mary set an example with her life that was worth paying
attention to. She could have been a lady of leisure as her husband
owned and operated a very successful business. Her home,
complete with white carpet and rich wood cabinetry, was a
showplace that could have been featured in a magazine. She was
an elder in her church, as well as a leader and active participant
in the Women's Society. She sent hundreds of greeting cards
to members and friends of the church, and regularly called on
the sick and the homebound. She counted it a privilege and
responsibility to greet newcomers in worship.

A lady of dignity and grace, she never let her dignity get in
the way of scrubbing the church office floor or cleaning up an
untidy restroom. She was a woman of faith who loved her Lord
and walked in His Way.

My prayer today, as I mourn the death of this dear friend, is that I will become more like Mary. Her walk in faith matched her words of faith. Even as her life was a blessing to me, I pray that my life will be a blessing to someone else.

> Together let us thank God for women of faith who have inspired us to become stronger in our faith.

Prayer

> Thank You, God, for the example and inspiration of my dear friend Mary. May I follow her example as I live out the days of my life. Amen.

WARM WELCOME
AT GETTYSBURG

Then answered Peter, and said unto Jesus,
"Lord, it is good for us to be here."
—Matthew 17:4 (KJV)

It was Sunday morning in Gettysburg, Pennsylvania, and I wanted to attend worship. I was tired from spending a week of vacation on crutches with a broken ankle; I needed the peace that could come only from God. Locating a church downtown on a busy corner, I painfully made my way up the six wooden steps. Halfway up, I questioned my decision to attend *this* church—until I reached the top step. The door slowly opened before me, and a gentleman in a gray suit, white shirt, and red tie welcomed me into the historic church. Another gentleman approached to hand me a bulletin and escort me to the sanctuary, making sure that I was comfortably seated.

The prelude began—"Sheep May Safely Graze" by Bach—and I felt myself relax as the beauty of the sanctuary seeped into my soul. Gone was the stress of having to watch every step I took on crutches and the sadness of missing out on seeing some of the historic tourist attractions.

For years I had waited to travel to Gettysburg to stand where Abraham Lincoln stood when he delivered his famous address. For years I had ached to walk the battlefield where so many lives had been lost. I had planned, scrimped, and saved with high hopes of visiting all the local landmarks, some of which were not possible for me to visit.

But on that Sunday morning I found something far more significant than any local landmark I could have visited. I found an inner peace in that historic church and its people. With the reading of God's Holy Word and the content of the pastor's message on God's love and redeeming grace, I was again reminded that no matter how I feel or where I roam, God is there before me. And as I struggled back down the front steps, the words of Peter, the disciple, were in my heart: "It is good for us [me] to be here."

Look for God everywhere, even while on vacation.

Prayer

> Thank You, Father, for dedicated Christians in that historic church that drew me into their family of believers and helped me experience the peace and comfort I was seeking. Amen.

THE SILENCE OF
DEATH VALLEY

Yea, though I walk through the valley of the
shadow of death, I will fear no evil.

—Psalm 23:4 (KJV)

As I stood in a field in California's Death Valley, I sifted a handful
of hot dusty sand through my fingers. I picked up a rock lying
nearby, only to instantly drop it because of the intense heat it
was giving off! And while the sand and the rock created lasting
impressions with their dryness and heat, what struck me most
while standing in the scorching afternoon sun was the total
absence of sound.

Alone. Never had I felt so alone for there was no sound to
be heard. Straining to hear a bird chirping, a leaf rustling in the
wind, or a dog barking nearby, my ears were filled only with the
sound of silence—total, overpowering, empty silence!

As this silence began to feel like a blanket that threatened to
smother me, a verse from the Twenty-third Psalm came unbidden
to calm me: "Yea, though I walk through the shadow of the valley
of death, I will fear no evil, for Thou art with me" (Psalm 23:4
KJV). Gently, yet forcefully, these words were a reminder that no
matter where I am, even in the middle of silent and desolate Death
Valley, I am not alone for God is there with me.

I am so glad that I consciously chose to have this "Death Valley" experience! I am glad I took the time to get out of the air-conditioned car to walk into the desert and stand in the desolate silence. For the memory of experiencing God in that "valley of the shadow of death" has stayed with me and often prompts me to move away from my busy schedule, ringing cell phone, and hectic lifestyle to seek God in a quiet place.

When have you stood in a quiet spot? Did you feel God there?

Prayer

> Thank You, God, for times of quietness when we become keenly aware of Your presence. Amen.

FINDING STRENGTH
FOR THE TASK

When thou passest through the waters, I will be with thee.

—Isaiah 43:2 (KJV)

"I don't know what to do, God!" I cried out as I drove to Wisconsin from Iowa. "I shouldn't have to be helping to plan my son's funeral! Sons are supposed to outlive their mothers. O God, I just don't know what to do!" Of course I cried and cried as each mile brought me nearer to the reality of the task before me. And over and over, I reminded God that I didn't know what to do.

Later that night, as sleep eluded me, I pulled out my Bible and randomly opened it, hoping to find a verse to give me some direction. And there, in the forty-third chapter of Isaiah, was God's promise to the Israelites that could have been written to me:

> But now the Lord who created you, O Israel, says: "Don't be afraid, for I have ransomed you. I have called you by name. When you go through deep waters and great trouble, I will be with you. When you go through rivers of difficulty, you will not drown … for I am the Lord your God, your Savior." (Isaiah 43:1–3 TLB)

As I sat there alone in that motel room in Wisconsin, I read these verses with eyes full of tears. And I knew that I was not alone. I knew I would have strength to do the things that had to be done because the Lord, my God, who called me by name, would be walking beside me. With these timeless words, God had reminded me that I was not alone, and I would not drown in the river of tears that I had cried or in the river of sorrow that swirled around me. I had the promise of the God I love and worship that He will be with me.

> When you feel most alone, open God's Word,
> and find strength for your journey.

Prayer

> Thank You, God, for promises written thousands of years ago that are so meaningful and comforting today. Help me to cling to these promises as I walk into the future. Amen.

COFFEE GROUNDS EVERYWHERE

My cup runneth over.

—Psalm 23:5 (KJV)

One of the last things I do before retiring for the night is set up the coffeepot for the next morning. By doing this, I only need push the button to begin brewing my morning cup of coffee. But a few days ago, something went dreadfully wrong! As I walked past the coffeepot soon after hitting the button, I saw water and wet coffee grounds all over the countertop. Quickly unplugging the pot, I began to clean up the mess, all the while muttering about modern-day devices that don't work right.

Imagine my chagrin when I discovered that while I had put the paper coffee filter in the coffee maker, and put the coffee grounds in the filter, I hadn't put the filter in the filter *basket* before putting it into the coffee maker. Because of this, the filter was just lying in the empty space where the basket belonged, allowing the water and coffee grounds to run rampant through the machine. The manufacturer had designed a great product; I failed to put all the pieces in place to brew a good cup of coffee.

Kind of like my spiritual life in many ways. When I don't install the filter of God's tolerance into my life, the streams of negativity and unhappiness with the actions of others can run rampant through the days of my life. For without the filtering process that comes with living as Jesus has taught me to live, I become obsessed with minor grievances and inconveniences and lose the big picture of God's love and forgiveness. It is only when my words and actions are filtered through the teachings and forgiveness of God that I live a life worthy of my calling as a disciple.

It truly makes a difference in living a life of faith if all the pieces of love, prayer, and forgiveness are put in their rightful places.

Prayer

> Dear Father, You have given me the tools of scripture and prayer to set up my spiritual life successfully. Help me to use these tools to touch other lives with Your love. Amen.

THE UNSIGNED POLICY

Go thy way for this time; when I have a
convenient season, I will call for thee.

—Acts 24:25 (KJV)

The application for life insurance was all filled out. The agent, the husband of one of her trusted friends, encouraged her to complete the process that cold March day by signing the application and leaving a check with him. He promised that he would lock the two in his filing cabinet until she called him with her final decision to purchase the policy. I have wondered many times in the years since that day why she hesitated. She could have done so with an easy conscience because they had been friends for many years. She knew that his word was his bond for she had done business with him in earlier times.

But she didn't.

And to this day, her hesitation haunts me. She had taken the time to fill in all the blanks and had even named her beneficiaries. She had answered all the health questions and had sufficient money in the bank to pay the premiums. But still, she asked for a few more days to think it over. And those "few days" proved very costly.

Just one week later, she lost her life in an automobile accident. Had she signed her name and completed the process, the insurance money would have paid for her daughter's college education.

Her hesitation opened my eyes to the many times I put off making important decisions. Sometimes my hesitation is justified. But more often than not, I am just reluctant to make a decision. It is then that I remember today is the only day God has given me. Tomorrow may not be mine to live.

Let us not put off until tomorrow what must be done today.

Prayer

> Help me, God, in each day of my life to make wise decisions in all areas of my life. Amen.

AND THEN IT RAINED

I will cause the shower to come down in his
season; there shall be showers of blessing.
—Ezekiel 34:26 (KJV)

It was 1988 in the Midwest, and we hadn't had any rain for months. The mighty Mississippi was running so low that towboats were tied off along the upper Mississippi shorelines, unable to navigate in the shallow waters; crops were dying in the fields. Politicians were calling this the worst drought since the Dust Bowl. And everywhere I went to make sales calls, people were talking about the lack of rain. It was mighty serious business, and we all knew it.

And then one afternoon, while sitting in an office in a small western-Illinois town, I heard the cry go up in the street below the office window. "Hey, it's raining. I just saw some raindrops falling!" People began to rush out of stores and offices to stand looking up at the sky, waiting for more raindrops to fall.

And they did. First a few and then a torrent of raindrops! Buckets and buckets of raindrops. Church bells rang! Fire engine sirens blared! And people on the sidewalks laughed, shouted, and clapped as they stood with friends and strangers alike, enjoying the feeling of rain on their faces even as their clothes were getting soaked.

How grateful I am that the God who sends rain to water the earth also sends "showers of blessings" to water my soul. May I show as much joy in receiving them as I did on that August day in 1988 when the rain fell.

Do you thank God for the "showers" in your life?

Prayer

> Dear Father, You know how much I love to feel the rain on my face. Help me welcome Your showers of blessing into my life as well. In Jesus's name I pray. Amen.

ABOUT THE AUTHOR

While growing up as a "preachers kid" in Iowa and Illinois, JudyAnn Krell Morse cultivated a strong faith in God. She served one year in Alaska as an American Baptist Home Missionary, and fourteen years on staff at a religious convention grounds. Her written devotions have appeared in The Secret Place; presently she is the pastor of a small congregation in downtown Burlington, Iowa, a position she has held for eighteen years. Married, she is the mother of eight grown children and step-children.

Printed in the United States
By Bookmasters